I have
DIABETES

I have DIABETES

Brenda Pettenuzzo
meets
Marcus Burrows
Photography: Chris Fairclough
Consultants: British Diabetic Association

FRANKLIN WATTS

London/New York/Sydney/Toronto

Marcus Burrows is ten years old. He goes to St. Bede's Primary School, Chadwell Heath. His mother, Vera, is a District Nurse. His father, Keith, is the Butchery Manager in a large supermarket. Marcus has a sister, Kerry, who is fourteen. Marcus has had diabetes for two years. The family lives in Chadwell Heath, Greater London.

Contents

©1987 Franklin Watts
12a Golden Square
LONDON W1

ISBN: 0 86313 561 7

Series Consultant: Beverley Mathias
Editor: Chester Fisher
Design: Edward Kinsey

Typesetting: Keyspools Ltd

Printed in Great Britain

The Publishers, Photographer and author would like to thank Marcus Burrows and his family for their great help and co-operation in the preparation of this book.

Thanks are also due to St Bede's Primary School, Chadwell Heath, King George's Hospital, Newbury Park and Redbridge Young Diabetics.

Brenda Pettenuzzo is a Science and Religious Education teacher at St Angela's Ursuline Convent School, a Comprehensive School in the London Borough of Newham.

Life before diabetes

"I was just the same as everyone else until I was nine years old."

Marcus was a normal baby in every respect. He went through all the stages that most babies go through. He caught many of the "normal" sort of illnesses that children get, such as colds, sore throats and German measles. Marcus quickly recovered from them. He used to do all the things that other boys and girls did. He used to eat anything he liked and as often as he liked!

The first signs

"I became ill and the doctor told us that I had diabetes."

Marcus had been running out of energy at football matches. He was losing weight. No one knew exactly what was wrong, until he began to be terribly thirsty. His mother had guessed by this time that he might have diabetes. They went to their doctor and Marcus had his urine tested. The test showed that his urine contained too much sugar. The doctor arranged for Marcus to be admitted to hospital.

**"My mum took me to the hospital the next day.
I stayed in for three days."**

When Marcus arrived at the hospital he put on his
pyjamas and got into bed. Then he had a blood test to
see how much sugar there was in his blood. The test
told the doctor who was treating Marcus, how much
insulin would be needed to keep the right amount of
sugar in his blood. After three days, his blood sugar
was at a safe level. Marcus then went home and back
to normal life – well, almost!

"The doctors and the nurses at the hospital told me all about diabetes and insulin."

In hospital, Marcus learned about his condition and how it was going to alter his life. He also learned that he didn't have to let it change things too much. He was told that he would need injections of insulin twice a day. He would have to watch just what he ate each day. Marcus would have to be sure that his food matched his insulin. For people with diabetes, too much food of the wrong type, or too much insulin, can be dangerous.

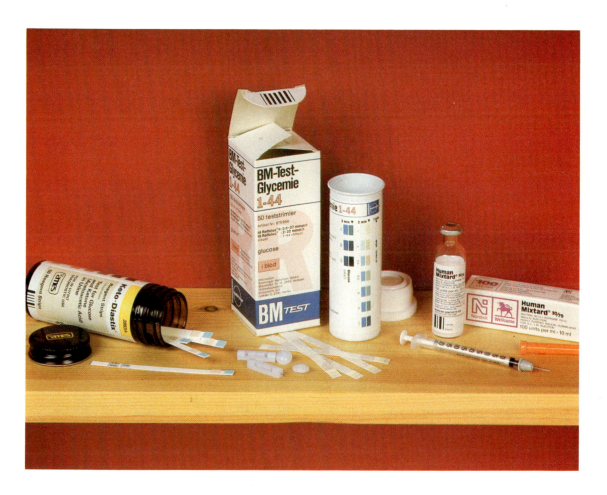

Living with diabetes

"I have to eat at regular intervals. This makes my sugar level stay nearly the same all the time."

Marcus has to eat several times during the day. His breakfast always includes cereal and toast, fresh orange juice and sometimes a boiled egg. He usually has a snack at midmorning, lunch, another snack in the midafternoon, and a cooked dinner at about 5.30 pm. If he is going to be doing a lot of exercise he eats more energy-giving foods. In the evening, at about 8.30 pm, Marcus has another snack of toast or crackers or something similar, before he goes to bed at about 9.30 pm.

"I have a book which tells me the energy values of all my foods."

It is important for Marcus to have a balanced diet. He must have the right amount of energy-giving foods. If he has too much carbohydrate, his blood-sugar level will become too high, just as it was when Marcus first became ill. Too little, and he will begin to feel faint, and might soon become unconscious. Eating food with lots of fibre is very important. The carbohydrates in such food are absorbed more slowly. His mother helps him to balance his carbohydrates against his insulin dose, with the help of the book.

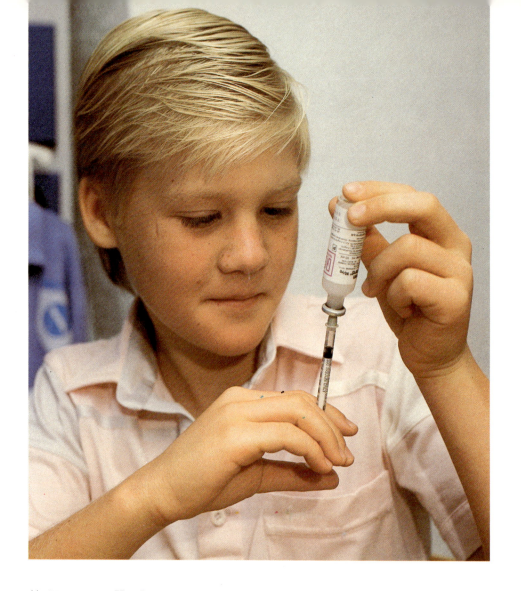

"We usually keep my insulin in a cool place. It's the first thing I think of in the morning."

Soon after he gets up, Marcus gives himself his insulin injection. He does this even before he has had anything to eat. He fills the syringe with the correct amount of insulin, and checks that there are no bubbles in it. Small children sometimes need help with their injections. Marcus gives himself his injections in the normal way.

"I choose a different place for each injection."

Marcus can choose to inject himself in his arms, thighs, calves, or his bottom! He chooses a different place each time so that he doesn't develop any sore places. He sometimes asks his mum to help if he wants to use a place which is awkward to reach. There are many different types of insulin. The doctor has chosen the one which is most suitable for Marcus. He gives himself his second injection at about 5.00 pm, half an hour or so before his evening meal.

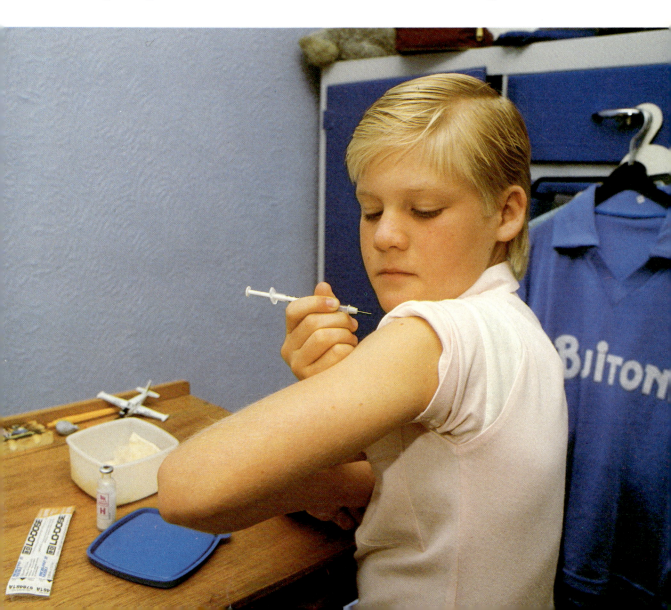

"I usually do a blood test each day."

Until a few years ago, most people with diabetes had to check their urine each day, to measure the sugar level. (When the level in the blood is high, it also shows up in the urine.) Now a simple blood test can measure sugar level directly. This method is very accurate. Marcus pricks his finger and puts a drop of blood on to a stick coated with chemicals. The chemicals change colour. A special machine converts the colour changes into a reading of the exact amount of sugar in the blood.

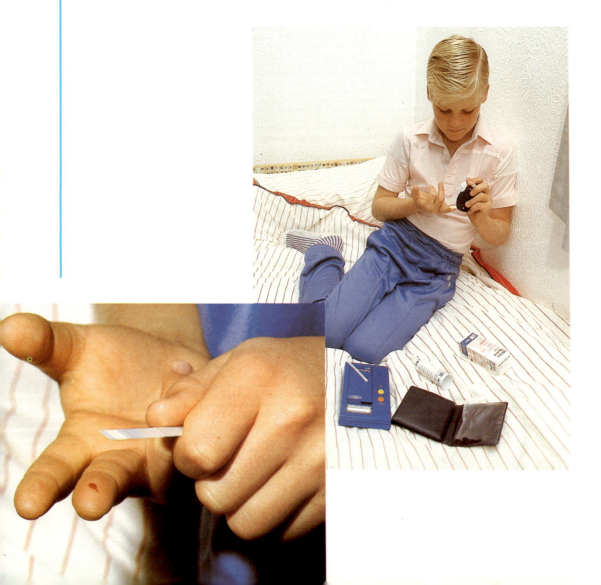

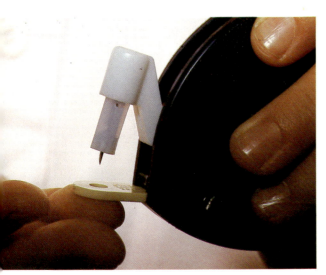

"I keep a record of my blood tests in a special diary."

Each day Marcus does his blood test at a different time. He notes down the results in a special diary. This makes it easy for him to build up a picture of the way in which his sugar level goes up and down, at different times of the day. He also gets to know what sort of things affect it. Sometimes it may seem very high for no obvious reason, but there is nearly always an explanation for any changes. He always does a blood test if he feels unwell in any way.

At school

"My teachers know that I have diabetes. It doesn't make any difference to the things I do at school."

It is important that Marcus' teachers know about his diabetes. If he were to faint or feel ill at any time, they would need to know what is the best thing to do. Sometimes he feels the need to eat before the normal time for morning snack. At such times his teacher will let him eat early.

"When I first had diabetes I sometimes used to feel 'strange'. Now I can do anything I want to do."

Most people with diabetes take a few months to settle down to their routine of insulin and diet. Now that Marcus has passed this early stage, he can join in all the sports and other activities at school. He always makes sure that he has had enough to eat, and he usually carries something extra. If his sugar level were to get low because of all the energetic things he does, he can always quickly eat something to raise it.

Playing sports

"I play football for two teams – my school and the Redbridge junior team."

Marcus spends a lot of his spare time training and practising. Marcus feels that he is playing better now than he did before he became a diabetic. Just before he became ill, he had been getting very tired. He was going to change his position to goalkeeper, so that he could stand about more!

"I like lots of sports. Apart from football, my favourite is swimming."

Marcus likes swimming with his friends and with his family, especially if the weather is hot and he can go to an open-air pool! Before going swimming, Marcus must be sure that he has had enough to eat. He also carries a supply of glucose with him in case he feels his blood sugar level going down. He also plays tennis, whenever he can persuade his dad or Kerry to play with him.

Warning signals

"I usually carry something sugary to eat, just in case I feel I'm becoming 'hypo'."

"Hypo" is the word people with diabetes use when they mean *hypoglycaemic*. This is a medical word which means that the sugar level in their blood has gone too low. This could be because they have missed a meal, or haven't eaten enough. Most people have their own warning sign when this is happening. Marcus usually feels dizzy. Other people feel sleepy, or get a "buzz" in the head, or get irritable.

"I have a card and a bracelet that say I have diabetes"

Many people who have a condition like Marcus carry some sort of identification with them all the time. If Marcus were to become ill, while away from home, anyone who sees the bracelet can open it and read details of his condition. He also carries a card which has the name of the hospital he goes to and the doctor he sees. In this way, his parents and doctors can make sure that he never receives the wrong treatment accidentally.

Check-ups

"I usually go to the hospital every three months for a check-up."

Although he would go to the hospital at once if there were an emergency, Marcus and his mum or dad visit the specialist for regular check-ups. In the first part of the visit a specialist nurse weighs and measures Marcus, to make sure that he is growing normally. The nurse chats to him while he does a blood test. They might discuss his blood sugar level, or how he has been feeling lately. Marcus then goes back to the waiting room, to be called for the next part of the visit.

"The doctor then examines me and looks at my diary."

The diary gives the doctor a guide to the health of Marcus during the last three months. The doctor and the specialist nurse always speak to Marcus himself, although his mother or father are there as well. They look at all the places where he does his injections, and ask about his general health. The doctor might also suggest that Marcus needs a different insulin dose, or that he could eat more. At the clinic they also make sure that Marcus is having regular eye examinations. It is a very friendly visit, and Marcus is never worried about going to the hospital.

Month: Jan 86.

Your doctor will advise you which tests you should perform.

Date	Insulin AM (Human Mixtard)	Insulin AM	Insulin PM (Human Mixtard)	Insulin PM	Blood Before breakfast	Blood 2hrs after breakfast	Blood Before mid-day meal	Blood 2hrs after mid-day meal	Blood Before evening meal	Blood 2hrs after evening meal	Blood Before bed	Blood During night	Urine Before breakfast	Urine Before mid-day meal	Urine Before evening meal	Urine Before bed	Comments
17	8		6		5.7												
18	8		6		5.3				10.2								Vomiting Am.
19	8		8					11.2					0				
20	8		8		6.2				3.7								Tummy upset
21	8.		6		3.9				5.2								Football Training. Hypo 9pm.
22	8		6		5.8				3.8						0		Back to School.
23	8		6								38		0				
24	8		6											0			
25	8		6		5.6		6.5										
26	8		6				7.2								0	0	Hypo 6.30pm.
27	8		6		7.7					6.7			0				
28	8		6						6.9							0	
29	8		6						8.5								
30	8		6		6.5										0	0	
31	8		6		7.1				6.3								

The Young Diabetics

"We heard about the 'Young Diabetics' soon after I got diabetes."

Quite a long time ago, some parents of diabetic children living quite near to Marcus, got together to form a group. They wanted to help each other and to find ways of helping their children. The children are now over twenty years old, but the group of parents still exists and is called the 'Redbridge Young Diabetics.' There are similar groups in other parts of the country. They do lots of different things.

THE TWENTIES
INSULIN DISCOVERE
THESE CHILDREN GIVEN LI

"We go to meetings every month. There are lots of other activities as well."

As well as having a monthly meeting where young people with diabetes and their parents can get together, there are plenty of fund-raising and social events to go to. Madeleine, the Diabetes Specialist Nurse, is usually there, and often a speaker who will talk about something interesting or important to people with diabetes. Parents of children who have only just become diabetics can talk to those who are 'old hands'. The group arranges swimming galas, and takes part in the local Carnival. The high spot of the year is, of course, the Christmas Party!

"This year I've had two holidays. One with the Young Diabetics and one with my family."

During the school summer holidays the British Diabetic Association holds Summer Camps for young diabetics. Marcus went to a camp in a boarding school in Kent, and enjoyed himself very much. There were outings and activities for everyone. Several doctors, dieticians and nurses stayed there with them. He has also been on holiday to Italy with his family. It was quite easy for him to work out what he should be eating each day, with a little help from his mum.

With the family

"We do lots of things together just like other families."

When Marcus' illness was first diagnosed, his family didn't know how they were going to treat him at home. They wondered whether he would be fussy and want a lot of attention. Now he behaves as if nothing had ever happened. He joins in the usual family activities and outings. No one treats him any differently from the way they treated him before.

Facts about diabetes

Marcus has a form of diabetes which is called **insulin dependent**. It usually affects children and young people and always has to be treated with injections of insulin. Older people sometimes get another type of diabetes, called **non-insulin dependent**, which can be treated with diet and tablets.

No one yet knows why people get diabetes, but doctors do understand how it happens and how to treat it. So far, no one has been able to prevent it or cure it.

Much of the food we eat is converted during the process of digestion into glucose, a form of sugar. This is carried by our blood to all parts of the body, where it is burned to give us energy. What we do not use for energy can be stored in the form of fat. Insulin is produced by a gland called the pancreas, and it circulates in the bloodstream, making it possible for glucose to enter the different types of cells and be used. We need to have a certain level of glucose in our blood all the time, and insulin controls this.

After every meal, the pancreas makes just the right amount of insulin to deal with the amount of glucose produced.

In people with diabetes, the part of the pancreas which makes insulin, stops working properly. When there is not enough insulin, all the glucose stays in the blood instead of being used up or stored. The sugar in the blood spills over into the urine, and the kidneys have to work extra hard to get rid of it. Glucose has to be diluted with lots of water, and so the person gets very thirsty. And because the sugar cannot be used in the normal way, the patient gets very tired and loses weight. Insulin injections can help to cope with the sugar, but they have to be combined with a careful diet. A normal pancreas releases insulin in response to the sugar level in the blood, but a diabetic has to organize his or her sugar levels to suit the insulin that is being injected.

There are now several varieties of insulin available, slow acting ones, fast acting, and mixtures of both. Various types of syringe can be used, and what is available varies in different parts of the world. Medical researchers are working hard in the field of diabetes, and new ways of giving insulin have been devised in the last year or so. There is a pump which can give small doses without the discomfort of using a

28

normal needle each time. Most diabetics use their needles without any fear at all, and small children of five years old have been known to give their own injections! Work is always underway to find a way of preventing diabetes, but so far doctors have been unable to do this or to predict which people are going to suffer from it. However, they are now able to prevent and treat many of the complications which used to affect most diabetics.

People with diabetes pay special attention to their eyesight, and their general health. They are careful to seek a doctor's advice if they have any infections, and they take care of cuts and sores which they might develop. Some people who have had diabetes for many years can develop complications. These affect the heart and blood vessels, causing eye and kidney problems, poor circulation and nerve damage. This only happens rarely nowadays because it is possible to keep their blood sugar level under much tighter control. Most diabetics grow up normally, go to work, have a family and take up careers in many fields. They do everything they would have done, if they had not become diabetic.

There are more than 600,000 people suffering from diabetes in the United Kingdom. 30,000 of these are children. It is believed that in the world there are about 30 million known cases of diabetes and another 30 million who have yet to be diagnosed.

About 70% of the known diabetics are probably only partially deficient in insulin. Many of those who are past middle-age are over weight, and just cannot make enough insulin to deal with their blood sugar. They can be treated with special diets (to lose weight) and tablets which stimulate their insulin production. The remaining 30% are dependent on insulin.

Insulin is obtained from the pancreas of pigs and cattle which have been killed for meat. Recently it has become possible to synthesize insulin so that it is exactly like the insulin produced by human beings. Most children with diabetes are now given this "human" insulin. Doctors are now able to prescribe insulin in various forms to suit each patient. There are slow- and quick-acting insulins which are often combined to give 24-hour cover, getting as close as possible to the natural situation in a person who has not got diabetes.

The British Diabetic Association

The BDA was formed in 1934 to help all diabetics. Its aims were to act as a means of communication for diabetics and professionals and to promote the study and proper treatment of diabetes.

These aims are still the same today, although the services provided have been greatly expanded.

Practical help and advice is provided to all diabetics and their families on all aspects of diabetes and a wide range of literature, books and videos is produced. Educational and activity holidays are organised for diabetics of all age groups plus weekends for families.

Throughout the UK, there are over 300 local branches and groups who hold regular meetings. They also provide support locally.

One of the major functions of the BDA is to support diabetic research. In 1987, over £1 million has been budgeted to support groups and projects who are all working to improve the treatment of diabetes and to find a cure for the disease and its complications.

Membership of the BDA is open to anyone – contact this address for details:

British Diabetic Association
10 Queen Anne Street
London W1M 0BD
Tel.: 01-323 1531

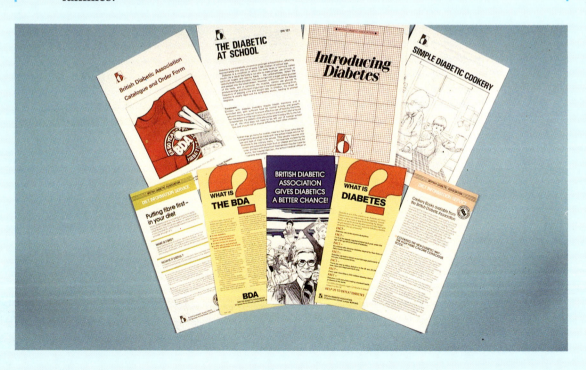

30

Glossary

Blood sugar The amount of glucose in the blood, which needs to be kept at a safe level all the time. Too little glucose, or, a low blood sugar, means that the brain will be starved of food. The diabetic will feel faint or shaky and may behave oddly. Sugar or glucose given by mouth, so long as the person can swallow, quickly corrects this situation.

Carbohydrates The category of food which includes sugars and starches. They are used by the body to provide energy. Excess carbohydrates can be changed into fat and contribute to over weight.

Diet This means the variety of foods which must be eaten in order to stay healthy. People with diabetes have to be aware of their diet all the time. Their diet is often a lot more healthy than that of many others, because they are encouraged to eat foods which are high in fibre, and low in many less healthy things like fat.

Fibre This is also called dietary fibre or roughage. It is the part of our food intake which we are unable to digest, such as the skins of fruits, cereals etc. Fibre is essential for the healthy working of the gut. Carbohydrates which are eaten in foods with a high fibre content are absorbed more slowly, causing a steadier rise in blood sugar level.

Glucose A simple sugar which is found in all living things. It is the final breakdown product of most carbohydrates during digestion. Excess fats and other substances can be broken down into glucose.

Hypoglycaemia This means "low blood sugar". The body needs to have a certain amount of sugar in the blood to be able to function properly. If the blood sugar levels fall too low then the person begins to feel strange and will be unable to do things properly. Hypoglycaemia can be remedied by taking some type of sugar.

Insulin A special type of chemical, called a hormone, produced in the Pancreas by special cells called the "Islets of Langerhans". Insulin controls the amount of glucose in the blood. Diabetes sufferers cannot produce insulin, or produce an insufficient amount.

Pancreas A gland which is found under the stomach in humans. It produces a digestive juice which is secreted into the gut, and insulin which is passed directly into the bloodstream.

Index